I Was Blind, but Now I See

Valerie Miller

WESTBOW
P R E S S®
A DIVISION OF THOMAS NELSON
& ZONDERVAN

WestBow Press books may be ordered through
booksellers or by contacting:

WestBow Press
A Division of Thomas Nelson & Zondervan
1663 Liberty Drive
Bloomington, IN 47403
www.westbowpress.com
1 (866) 928-1240

ISBN: 978-1-5127-0899-8 (sc)
ISBN: 978-1-5127-0900-1 (e)

Library of Congress Control Number: 2015913451

Print information available on the last page.

WestBow Press rev. date: 11/10/2016

Not what I expected

In this journey called life, I have been surprised, disappointed and mislead. How? you may ask. How can that be when you were following God's instructions? I waited and waited for what was told to me, kept the faith and when the appointed time arrived I didn't receive or did I? I couldn't understand it, I asked myself, why is it this way? I did everything I was supposed to do. I obeyed leadership. I delighted myself in the Lord. I loved the Lord thy God with all my heart, soul and mind. I loved my neighbor as myself. I didn't forsake the assembly of others. I placed on the whole armor of God. I kept my expectation up. Then it dawned on me...I lacked one important thing. Patience. Patience is not a strong suit. Strong suit? Are you even putting it on? And on top of that, it was in seed form. I expected it to be a finished product. Just go right on in and possess the land, but it was not so. I had to toil the land, work the seed in the dirt, plant it, water it, and wait for it to grow.

I didn't mind a little hard work, hey I welcomed it. I'm that type of chick that enjoys working with her hands. Dirt in between my fingernails, calloused hands, mud on the face, none of those things bother me. Even crawling underneath something to get the job done is quite interesting and exciting, just show me the way and teach me as we go along. Dirt, mud, grass, cement, sand... it doesn't matter I'm along for the adventure. But there is one I never tried but look forward to the day...Look at you, you can't wait to hear it. After a great down pour of rain...I'm talking sheets of rain coming down heavy. I would even welcome a little lightening and thunder where there is nothing but red dirt preferably. You get where I'm driving at? :) Driving through the mud in a pickup truck or the jeep that has no protection like windows... sighing with contentment and joy. Especially if it is in the south, the combination of hot weather and cool water. Revving those tires and swirving every which way...mud slinging and splashing everywhere. Your face, arms, legs and vehicle covered in loose mud...a contented sigh escapes me, oh man. Now don't think me to be in the pig family, I like cleanliness. It is just something about nature; the smell of fresh cut grass, listening to crickets at night, the smell of rain coming, picking up slugs when they are in protective mode...their horns come out. Mud, walking in the sand, lightening, thunderstorms... oh my gosh, I love a good thunderstorm. And don't let it be a hurricane...you name it I love it. And lets not talk about laying on the ground... have you ever done it? You've got to try it, there is this peace like no other. Just look up into the sky and let everything go, there is nothing like it. No worries, no problems, or concerns...its just you and peace. Then you will understand me when I say that its a favorite past time. You will get more out of it if you tune your ears to hear the earth around you; like the birds, the wind blowing, the laughter of children...now that's living. I caught a geicko like that one day, rather he caught me but that's another story. So getting back to what I was saying earlier, <u>it takes work</u>...whatever it is, building, growing, and cleaning...mud especially. Don't let it dry up on you, there is no fun in that...now that will take effort. But that's why God made soap and water. When you're done playing, clean it up.

The next step was wait, I waited this long why not wait some more. I was still experiencing the joy of receiving, working and getting my hands dirty. Come on, all I have to do is wait. How hard is that? Very hard, extreemly hard but it doesn't have to be. It's just plain old trust. Let patience have it's perfect work that you will be complete and entire wanting nothing. I want to be complete and entire, hey, who am I kidding we all want that. So if I trust you than I can wait for it, right? Countless times I have read many things and these words rang out so strong, "You are in need of patience," but I expected that to be done quickly as well. Back to the drawing board...It's more than quoting scripture, it's applying it everyday. <u>No matter how long it takes and how often it takes</u>. If I have confidence in what you are saying to me, and in your word than it should not be a problem. Is there a problem? I'm beginning to see that it is but it's not in God but in me. I'm the problem,"Ouch!" So the real question is... Do you believe the words that is coming out of His mouth? Even though it is not right away, do you believe what God told you? His word is good seed and good seed bring forth good fruit. Fruit comes from trees and not plants. Fruit trees take about five years to grow. Seeds don't grow right a way when they are plants, and now that I know it is a tree. Can you wait for it? It takes time...will you wait for it?

Foundation

Depending on the ground work, and to what was left behind. Have you ever had to clean up behind someone else? And so it may take longer than we expected. The process begins with removing weeds, broken branches, dead leaves, pebbles, rocks, glass particles, papers, cardboard, soiled foods, gathering and disgarding trash brought on by the winds and storms of life. Breaking into the earth, turning the dirt over, and just to find more buried trash. Years and years of garbage that was hidden all this time you thought was gone begin to show face. So...you start the process all over again. Removing old roots, and other people's garbage, turning the dirt once again and again until it's time to plant the seed or seeds, depending if you want a harvest. And don't be surprised, you will be visited by the strangest creatures during this time of obstruction, I say obstruction because you will be the intruder. Tearing down their security, establishments, and restaurants...restaurants you're questioning. You will be surprised what we eat every day. What people say, what we say to ourselves and what we read on a daily basis. Their inquisitive minds ask, what's all this fuss about? Who hired the demolition worker and why are they destroying our home? Some may come up to your face boldly and others may buzz a few words in your ears. Swapping away the talk you continue to work. Reminded of the repelent you placed on before you began your work, you relax and become thankful that the power is still effective. Placing on the whole armor of God doesn't stop them from coming but prevents them from harming. Remember, No weapon formed against you shall prosper. It will be formed and sent out but won't succeed at destroying you. The outside interferences are held at bay.

Yes, it is a process, and process means time, effort, energy, enthusiasm, endurance, faith, determination, tenacity, long-suffering, willingness, patience and more patience. And sad to say moments of distress...weariness may come along for the visit as well. But that's everything in life. I'm beginning to see that now and although I would like to change a few things, I can't. I just have to accept it, the only thing I can change is myself. Somethings are just not meant to be changed and so embrace it. Is it easy? No, but doable. I'm beginning to see patience as a friend and no longer an enemy. Like a toddler in the toy store, "I want it now! Now, now!" After you have asked all the questions, pouted, through the tamptrum, stretched out on the floor,sighed long enough and balled your fist, you are now at acceptance. Accepting that waiting is a virtue. Just to think, it took all that dirt for me to see that. If it wasn't for the dirt I wouldn't have grown to know that God has so much in store for me. I didn't need all those things I tried to keep. Buried trash is treasures to some of us. We don't want no one to find it more or less know about it. And giving it to God is not easy either but it must be done. He sees the treasure but it's not treasure at all, it's poison that will kill you in the longrun and all those that would eat of your garden.

Now there is such a thing called good dirt... miracle grow. It would take a miracle for you to grow. God still works miracles in our lives, **if we let him**. Hard dirt, cold dirt, muddy, gossip, he say, she say, they say, you say, *swing your partner dosey doe, snatch the handle off the door. Just a little square dance humor there.* And if you want prosperous fruit you would include the compose. Compose is disgarded food no one eats... more or less touch...You mean keep the remains but you just said throw it away. Only keep the good stuff. That's if you want to grow strong and healthy. But it stinks. Yes it does but it caused you to get closer to God. That compose increased your prayer life. What is that verse... And we know that all things worked together for the good for those that are the called according to his purpose. Yes it looks bad but it is good for you. I was listening to one of Bishop Jakes sermons and he spoke about the things you learn along the way. Things you have learned along the way to the destiny God has for you will determined your next move. If you throw it away, you may wind up going through it again, and if it was very painful the first time around... you might want to remember the lesson you have learned. The bible says to abhor that which is evil and cleave to that which is good. The older ones say, "Eat the meat and spit out the bones."

So when you hear, "animal dung, egg shells, nut shells, and fruit peelings, you automatically squish your face and say throw it away. But that's just what we need to grow healthy plants and trees. These are refused items that no one wants more or less touch and handle yet we need them to grow strong. Have you've been a refused item in life...was you a throw away? Well God has use for you in His kingdom. I need you to help me grow and vise of versa, you need me to help you grow. He said in John 6:12 (Guideons) "So when they were filled, He said to His disciples, gather up the fragments that remain, so that nothing is lost." Fragments are broken pieces, the pieces people throw away. Broken pieces can be your dreams, broken promises, broken hearts, broken relationships, and what often takes place when there is brokenness there comes harm. Broken glass can harm you if you are not careful while holding it. It cuts and wounds others too. Have you ever heard the saying, hurt people hurt other people. Well it's true, although not intentionally. But I have good news, Psalms 51:17 (KJV) "The sacrifices of God are a broken spirit: a broken and a contrite heart, O God, thou will not despise." (Psalms 147:3) "He healeth the broken in heart, and bindeth up their wounds." (Isaiah 61:1, 2, 3) "The spirit of the Lord is upon me: because the Lord hath anointed me to preach good tidings unto the meek, He hath sent me to bind up the broken hearted, to proclaim liberty to the captives, and the opening of the prison to them that are bound." "To proclaim the acceptable year of the Lord, and the day of vengence of our God, to comfort all that mourn." "To appoint unto them that mourn in Zion, to give unto them beauty for ashes, the oil of joy for mourning, the garment of praise for the spirit of heaviness, that they might be called trees of righteousness, the planting of the Lord, that He might be glorified." (Isaiah 61:7) "For your shame ye shall receive double, and for confusion they shall receive their portion, therefore in their land they shall possess the double: everlasting joy shall be unto them."

You see He came to seek and save the lost. We may have lost all hope and ended up into the lost and found quite a few times in life but who was the main one that found us...Christ. We may have found ourselves lost but there was only one that could bring us out and it's Jesus. We can't save ourselves, we all need a Savior. No matter the status, age, creed, and color...we all need a Savior and thank God it has already been established. God sent His Son to die <u>for all humanity</u>. Who would have thought... One man dying...not just any man, the Son of man. God in the flesh died for you and I, and all we have to do is believe the work he has done on the cross and we shall live forever with him. Saved, rescued, and delivered...our bail has been paid in full and all we have to do is walk out of that prison a free person. But it's staying out of prison that takes work, and that's our part to do. Be not entangled in the yoke of bondage again to fear. Let us look at Romans 10: 9, 1 (KJV) "That if thou shalt confess with thy mouth the Lord Jesus, and shalt believe in thine heart that God hath raised him from the dead, thou shalt be saved. For with the heart man believeth unto righteousness and with the mouth confession is made unto salvation." So are you saying just acknowledge that I need God in my life and tell Him so, and I shall receive eternal life? Yes, but the most important of all... you must believe it. Without faith its impossible to please Him. Once planted in the soil, the next phase is death. Anything buried will die but then it will live again.

Disappointment

Just starting out as a gardener, I guess you can call me an apprentice. Didn't know much about it but I've looked on and assisted in sowing and putting down fresh soil for others. It looked pretty easy and I desired to plant my own flowers, fruits and vegetables. I asked a few questions here and there and got on the move. Not forgetting my compose batch, miracle grow soil, plant food and all my gardening tools, I planted good seeds and began to see sprouts, happy with glee to come out the next day, I planted some more. Some plants grew faster than others and some remained dormant. Not losing hope, I began to see fruition. Watering my garden like I was instructed to do, rejoicing and praising my God, I continued the process. Like any first fruit, you tithe, share and eat. The first crop was green beans, I was more than excited I was ecstatic, more fruit arrived. I noticed how fresh my vegetables tasted, and it was good to know they came from my hand. Than the inevitable happened, I started to see perfectly digged holes in the ground and scattered vegetables. I was like, What in the world? I couldn't figure it out, it rained alot that season but I couldn't believe the rain did it and so I would replant the discards and gone back to my first works. Then one day drawing back my curtains to let the sun in the house, looking out the window I found the theives...it was a squirrel and some birds. I had no idea that squirrels were into compose and could smell it under ground to boot. My plants were dying because I was unaware of what came along with the process. I was discouraged, sadden and asked myself what didn't you do that you were supposed to? I followed the instructions, and then I remembered that someone told me to drop canyon pepper around my flowers to keep back the intruders. It's not just sowing the seed into the ground and moving along, more comes along with the dream, and the desire. It's like wanting to make a dish you have seen in a cook book or on a calendar with recipes and realized that you didn't have all the ingredients but you still wanted to make the dish. Well that was me, I didn't have all the ingredients and yes you guessed it...still lacking that patience. Isaiah 66: 8, 9 comes to mind, "Who hath heard such a thing? who hath seen such things? Shall the earth be made to bring forth in one day? or shall a nation be born at once? for as soon as Zion travailed, she brought forth her children." "Shall I bring to birth, and not cause to bring forth? saith the Lord: shall I cause to bring forth, and shut the womb? saith thy God." I wanted to do it anyway. Every seed is not the same and grow in different seasons. So I was discouraged for nothing but I had to learn that lesson along the way. Not too much water, not too much sun, and get the canyon pepper. Was it meant to be... was I a gardener or just a sower? Now don't misunderstand me...both positions have great rewards but was I just thinking about the work, the time, the effort, and the energy for it to just die. Some plant, some water but God gives the increase. It caused me to reflect back to the parable Jesus gave about the sower in the book of Matthew 13:3-23, when you get the chance read it for yourself. There was a lesson in all of this, first natural than spiritual. I had to wait for God and remembering that we can not do nothing without Him.

Dying to live again

Have you ever heard someone say, "I just want to live." They have crossed through so many obstacles in life and they just want to live. Well in order to live you have to die. What, have to die? Who said anything about dying? I said that I want to live. Live the good life. Yeah, and in order to do that, you have to die. Your old habits, your old ways, old patterns, point blank I had to die...but I love myself. Love thy neighbor as thy love thyself. Why did I have to die? I didn't want to die but what God has for you and I, we have to die. Anything dead does not feel. Dead things do not react. An issue that raised your blood pressure in the past or took you out of character wouldn't raise to life in the future... **if it is dead**. Bishop Jakes said, "If it's dead in your mind it's dead in your life." Dying is not easy. Dying means letting it go. Dying means surrendering. Have you heard the statement, " Let go and let God." Easier said than done yet we quote it for others to follow. But forget to be the first partaker. And I have, it wasn't easy... and would you believe I had to do it over and over again? Surrendering all my rights, my will, my patterns, and my way. Submission...We hear that lovely word when someone is taking the big step of marriage and now we are here having this conversation. Giving up, stop fighting... when I first heard those words. I didn't see where I was fighting God but then later on in my walk I was able to see what he was saying. I planned my life, well in my mind I did. My life was planned before the foundation of the world and I had nothing to do with it although I was in it. I just had to surrender to God's and disguard my own plans. Simple.

We make plans for our lives? Yes, we do but God says, I know the thoughts I have for your life, thoughts of good and not evil. To give you hope and an expected end. And although I thought mine was good enough, God's was higher. So naturally I had to give up. It sounds like I gave up immediately, right? I didn't. It was a long, long, long ways to go. I had to trust Him all over again. This time around, death was involved. Even though we have knowledge of Jesus being the ressurrection, we still find it hard to die. Well you just don't know what I had to go through and experience...that's what made me strong. And sad to say but that eventually made our hearts dead and cold inside. We got stronger and kept our guard up but it also caused us not to feel. What God has in mind is to give us a heart transplant and this heart will cause you to love and forgive. I had to read alot of love and forgiveness scriptures, and now beginning to study them. Reading and studying are two different things, reading is just gathering information, studying is requiring a change...making a difference. *"But you don't know what it cost me...the blood, sweat and tears."* I can imagine. We all had our moments but what I've found that when I let it die and although it was a slow death. My life changed, I mean really changed. Remember the scripture with Apostle Paul saying forgetting those things that are behind you and pressing toward the mark of the high calling? Philipians 3: 13, 14 (Gideons) "Brethren, I do not count myself to have apprehended, but one thing I do, forgetting those **things** which are behind and reaching forward to those those **things** which are ahead. I press toward the goal for the prize of the upward call of God in Christ Jesus." But that was an everyday agenda, he said we must die daily and it worked. I couldn't remember my past...I'm not pulling your chain here. It changed so much, I couldn't remember anything. It was sort of like amnesia, everything was new. I had to learn all over again but this time I was learning the good. This time around, I want to bear good fruit and in order for that to happen, and to continue to take place in my life, I had to be planted in good soil. Get plenty of the Son of God, be watered by the word of God, and stay rooted in Him. Some plant, some grow but God gives the increase.

Notice that I emphasized on the word things, because through the years in my walk with the Lord people came to mind not things. Hurt causes you to go there but the scripture didn't say people, it said things. How can we forget people when people are God's heart? Knowing that He conquered death, I still didn't yield to the idea. My dreams had to die in order for them to live again. My old mindset had to die in order to have God's thoughts. For without God we could do nothing and although these dreams came from the almighty, my old thoughts were coming along for the ride. How can two walk together except they agree? They can't, God wasn't in agreement with how things were going in my life and there had to be a change, that change consisted of me dying. Now that is a thought, I knew it wasn't going to be easy yet all I had to do was let go. It didn't require patience, it required trust. Is trust easy? No, it's not but is required. Faith, trust, and belief...all these words take action. Action is work, something **you** have to do. But it is not tedious work. It is just a made up mind. We can accomplish any task when we make up our minds to do so. And to keep it positive, we have to keep positive thoughts, and killing the negative. How do we kill negative thoughts? Making the exchange...throw out the bad and replacing it with the good. Philipians 4: 8 (Gideons) " Finally brethren, whatever things are true, whatever things are noble, whatever things are just, whatever things are lovely, whatever things are good report, if there is any virtue and if there is any praiseworthy, meditate on these things." Read, study, meditate, ponder on the word of life and most importantly...put it on. Apply it to your life every day, speak life to yourself, faith comes by hearing and hearing the word of God. Read aloud and slow to catch every word God is saying to you. His word brings life, joy and peace. Read great testimonies of what God has done for others, He is the same yesterday, today and forever more...what He has done for others He will do for you. Although His methods change, He doesn't change. Listen to inspirational music, pray and find yourself a bible based church and by all means do something different and fun. That is a plus... life is serious but also invigorating. There are so many things we could do and learn. Assemble yourself with positive people that will make you grow, challenge you, and keep you in the right spirit. Do things that give you joy, laugh, love, watch a few animated movies, do what you love...and live again.

The waiter

His yoke is easy and His burden lite. Learning about the restaurant business first hand, on the outside looking in seems simple but it is not, not by along shot. This is hard work people...you are on your feet all day, rushing to get things done in a fast pace environment, remembering an order, orders may change at the drop of a hat, you have to keep your composure at all times, and endure whatever comes along the way for everyday is not the same. And so looking at the waiter we see that everyone in this example is the waiter: the customer, the host and the chef; all parties have to stop, look and listen. The waiter have to stop and listen while the customer gives their order. The customer have to stop and listen to what the waiter has on the menu although they have read it for themselves and find out how it is prepared. Both parties have to listen attentively and take turns while they wait for the outcome. They have to be patient to hear without interrupting and when a question is asked of the preparations, the waiter have to able to answer to the best of their knowledge. The patron maybe allergic to the ingredients in the dish, by listening, the waiter is able to explain so there is clear communication and understanding before the meal is prepared. If the desire has somehow changed, there is another wait. More patience is required to hear the next request but they are doing it together. The chef receives the order and begins the process of preparing the meal. Clear communication, understanding, patience and doing things together causes things to become easy. His yoke is easy because you are not in this alone. God said that He will never leave you nor forsake you, He will be with you even to the end of the world. The burden is lite because He is carrying it with you. So after we ask, we have to wait and listen to what God has to say. *Well how do I know what He is saying?* Good question, you find out what He is saying by reading His word. *How do I know God is saying it and not my own ideas?* Because He agrees with His word and will always have a witness for you. Have you ever had a comfirmation? That is your witness, especially if the person He is using knows nothing of what is going on. That is when you know it is God and not a person. All the answers to lifes questions is in His word but you have to read to know it. And news flash people...the devil uses scripture too so be careful. Although he uses it, his agenda is different. He uses it as a trap or to bind you up, he twists the meaning or waters it down. He uses it nonetheless. Remember after Jesus got baptized by John the baptist, the bible says that He was led up into the wilderness by the Spirit to be tempted of the devil. The devil tempted Jesus with scripture, so if he did it with Jesus, he will do it with you. No servant is greater than his master. And so going back to the example of the restaurant business, food, time, patrons, money, character, and energy are saved. All participants have a special and important role to play in the industry. No one loses out, the customer may come again on several occassions, and recommend others to grow the establishment. So waiting plays a role in everything we do in life. Rushing usually causes a mess, an upset, mistakes and frustration. Patience can be a relative and not just a friend. Psalms 27:14 (Guideons) "Wait on the Lord, be of good courage, and He shall strengthen your heart: wait I say on the Lord!" Psalms 33:20 "Our soul waits for the Lord, He is our help and our shield." Psalms 37:34 "Wait on the Lord, and keep His way, and He shall exalt you to inherit the land: when the wicked are cut off, you shall see it."

Stop, look and Listen

I'm in my promise but where is the joy? Wait for it....wait for it.... wait for it. I'm in my promise but why is it still work, and harder now that it is mine? You know what I've always thought? After you've made it to your destination, the fight would be over but I was wrong. You still have to fight...fight to keep it, fight to maintain it and fight the good fight of faith. Now I see the real deal, now I hear the real deal and thanks be to God I got my joy back. What caused me to be down was the devil devices, he doesn't want to see you joyful but he is a liar. We know that no weapon formed against us will prosper. It was formed alright and even was shot with perfect aim **but** it backfired. Glory to God! The joy of the Lord is my strength. Reflecting back to this song Vanessa Bell Armstrong made, one of the verses said, "You can't hold me...so don't even try it." Anything in the beginning takes work, and even if it is something that you enjoy doing. So don't despise small beginnings. Going back to the waiter...patient, attentive, memory, stand, wait, serve, take notes, collect, bring, goes, does, quick, and receives...Stop? Look and listen? Where am I in pre-k? Yes and no...You are in school and class is in session. These are the basics we use in everyday life. So please take out your notebooks and start on the "Do now." Do it now and not later, do you know that the do now has alot to do with the homework? If you woud take a closer look, it is the actual lesson that will bring you through life without complications. And If you are struggling with the do now and decide to skip it, you will struggle all through the year, in every life lesson, your spiritual life, your home life, married life, and even your financial life. Go figure huh? But it is just "Do now"...hmmm is it? So now that you are aware...you have the opportunity to ask questions to get a better understanding so when the time comes for you to work alone, you will be able to go to the next level. So while the professor calls the names in the roll book you have to be attentive to listen for your name or you will be marked absent. Pay attention in class, the school of life can be very expensive. So while you are taking the notes down in your ledger, it pays not to talk in class or you will be written up depending on the grade level. James says, be quick to hear, slow to speak and slow to wrath.

It is a cost to get up early in the morning when you want to lie in bed, it is a cost to study when you prefer to watch movies or a television program. Discipline is a cost and it is not cheap by a long shot. Attendance, showing up, and being on time has alot to do with your grade, (performance, obedience, and respect.) Who is the one grading us? Life. Jesus is the way, the truth, and the life. Study to show ourself approved <u>unto God</u>, a workman need not be ashamed rightly dividing the word of truth. I use to think that there was no joy in school other than the first week, but I was wrong. It is joy when you begin to understand the work. What is required of you and when it is fully explained. It all has to do with you, what do you want out of this course? After that, the real work begins; pop quizzes, tests, exams, studying, homework, classwork, examples, ensamples, explaining your work, standing before the class, participation, speech and the final exam. Are you reading the notes? Are you reviewing the lessons? Are you spending quality time in the text book? If you are struggling, are you taking up on getting a tutor? A tutor is a person that has overcome the area you're struggling in. Are we alert or sleeping in class? Are we there altogether or just in body? Are we in a class all by ourselves or is the room full? Is there room for improvements?

Steps to take in order to pass: Show up, bring all required materials, be alert, sit up straight, listen for the instructions, follow the instructions, keep up with the class, don't leave and go ahead of the class assignment. Do the assignments together, help another student that is struggling to keep up when allowed to do so, especially if you were recommended. Now if you have helped that student and they refused to listen to you, that is not on you but on them, that is out of your control. When the time comes to take the test relax and be confident. <u>Confidence comes when you have done the work, for there is no need to fear</u>. You will pass the class. But this is a prerequisite for all subjects, all classes, and for all levels. When there is no longer a challenge it is time for you to go to the next grade and we begin the process all over again. Every row goes higher and higher. Remember the first week of school? The teacher would review what you have learned in your last grade to see where you are presently? You know, your strengths and weaknesses, cognitive skills; it is the same way in our christian walk. First natural than spiritual.

Phases and seasons

Remember the heinz catchup commercial? Anticipation is making me wait, soooo goood. But that doesn't exist in this world anymore, everything is instant, microwaveable, drive thru, automatic teller machine and somehow some of us have adopted to that same mode in our christian walk, I know I have but God is a God of patience. He doesn't have a problem of telling us to wait or say nothing at all. (Psalms 1: 3) "And he shall be like a tree planted by the river of water, that bringeth forth fruit <u>in his season</u>; his leaf also shall not wither; and whatsoever he doeth shall prosper." Are we looking at the right season? Or am I in someone else's season? Did I miss my season? How often does my season come around? Do you know your season? Have you ever worn something that was out of season? Either it was too hot or too thin, the season changed and so I have to go along with the season. This is my season for grace and favor and not everyone is going to be happy for your season. I had to learn that this year but it doesn't matter what another thinks... what do you think? What does God think? He thinks good toward me, and I think good towards Him. God is a good God all the time. And so I'm rejoicing for my season, this phase in my life. I thank God for new mercy and grace every morning. He allows me to live and learn in every stage of my life. I'm growing praise God... what was that verse Marvin Sapp sang, "I'm stronger, wiser, better, much better." Be instant in season and out of season, be quick to catch on. This is God's doing and it is marvelous in my eyes. The blessings of the Lord maketh rich and addeth no sorow. I am no where sorry...not at all. Thank you Jesus.

Genuine or Clitche'

"Good morning" Do you mean for me to have a good morning or is it just a greeting? "How you doing?" Are you really concerned? Will you wait for the response or walk on? "Whenever you need me I'm here." Whenever is not determined, so when that time arrives are you there for me in sincerity or it was just the normal logo? "Praise the Lord" Praise is an action not a greeting, hello is a greeting. Or good day but not praise the Lord. Is that individual or you dancing and leaping for joy? Are we both clapping our hands or lifting up His name, for that will be praising Him."God bless you." Do you really want God to bless me or you got so use to people saying that after someone sneezes. "I love you." Now that's a famous one. Do you really love me or you just want me to do something for you? "Well don't let me keep you" Are really saying get lost?

"Help yourself." But when the person begins to help themselves they receive the cross look and are talked about badly. Are you listening to the words that are coming out of your mouth? Something to think about, are these things from the heart or have I been accustomed to the everyday mundane conversation. Will I be judged for my words and not just deeds. Judgement begins at the house of God, I don't want my words to be in vain. The verse about let your yea be yea and nay, nay is beginning to make sense and take root.

Sow it

Why do we clinch tight to something that is already ours? The word of God says, The earth is the Lords the fullness thereof, the world and them that dwell therein. It also says that all are ours. As well as we are joint heirs with Christ. What is Christ's is ours because we belong to Him. Well this applies to those that have accepted the work He has done on the cross and received Him as Lord of their lives. If we do not belong to the family of God we do not have any claims. So I finally get it, letting go is opening my hand and laying the seed in the earth. Not only does this please our Father but it also springs forth new life for those abroad. A small seed that has expanded so wide that it can feed the five thousand and more so just as Jesus did with the young lads lunch. The meal that was prepared for this young child was sufficient for him but was sowed into the lives of others. Who would have thought two fish and five loaves of bread would go so far and beyond? That was a sacrifice, to give your lunch away. Yet he was willing, and Jesus received it. Lifted it up to heaven and blessed it. What God blesses can't no man curse. I say it again, **what God has blessed no man can curse**. Sacrifice is a willingness on our part not someone taking it away. Now if you take notice, the young lad didn't protest when one of the disciples suggested his lunch. Is someone suggesting your seed? What thoughts went through this little boys mind? We had a saying when I was coming up, "Children are to be seen and not heard." But that doesn't exempt what he felt.

You feel a sacrifice, sowing a seed is sacrifice. You go through a lot of stages when it comes to sacrificing something that is ours, that we have grown to love. Something that we enjoyed, have memories of...no, sacrifice is not a selfish act by no means necessary. Easily releasing something is not a sacrifice. A sacrifice is when you have nothing left and you are trying to make the best of what is. There are times we don't understand especially when God gave it to us in the first place, and now wishes for us to hand it to Him. This reminds me of Abraham, it was a sacrifice to willingly give up his son, he waited years to receive from the Lord and now God wanted him to sacrifice him. But God wanted to know if Abraham still loved him, even though the son had been a long waited promise. Abraham gave his son to God and God gave him right back. I had to give up something I received from the Lord, and just like he did with Abraham, He gave it right back to me. You see no one can take what God gave you, I had struggled with that for years. Why and how? Listening to what other people said and not taking heed to what God said. But going back to the word of God and really looking at Him. Studying everything about Him, He has every intention to bless His children. Reflecting on everything He told me to do concerning the gift, told me the outcome, showed me the outcome... Yet I still had a problem with giving it to Him. Now looking at it all, I can admit, I didn't trust Him. He kept saying that to me at different times but I kept reassuring Him that I did. Wow, isn't it amazing what God does in our lives? The lessons we learn when it is just a one on one tutor teaching us. It was never about me giving up something I worked hard on fixing up. It was all about my love to Him. To love someone takes trust...it's a risk to give your all to someone. That is the sacrifice, I'm sacrificing my heart in this relationship. You could hurt me but when it is love you are giving your heart to, He won't hurt you. I see God more and more in my life, and it's amazing.

So all that confusion that stirred up was to see what was in my heart in the first place, just like He did with Abraham. It was never about the people involved, the voices, the comments, the threats, it was always about the two individuals involved in that relationship. Now really looking at Him, what really matters is what He tells you...not what Sally or Joe says. I respect Sally and Joe but what matters the most is the one I'm in covenant with....His authority counts and is stronger than them all. You do what He says. Have you ever been in a situation where everyone is saying something but what really matters is what you say about it? I find myself in that place alot...sometimes it's hard to answer a question because my every word is being recorded. And although my intentions is not to bring harm, someone gets hurt. Let your yea be yea and our nay be nay. Starting to take that advice more and more...

and there is another one, no comment. So after I gave it, it was out of my mind. I didn't dream it, fret over it, cry for it...it was completely out of my mind and then months down the line, God gave it back. You see it was always mine, He was just getting my attention back on Him. And looking at Him the way He wants me to nothing else matters. Life has been added, there is increase, joy unspeakable and full of glory, and this is just the beginning. What God gives is not to consume us but to give us joy, and bring Him glory. It had me, I didn't have it. It had me stressed out, getting sick, aggrivated, upset, all the things that weren't in His plan in the first place.

For He knows all of His children, He knows the number of the hairs on our head. He knows our hearts. He knows what will cause us to fall and what will cause us to grow. Our Father knows it all, so when we finally comply and the act is done, there is such a peace that comes along with obedience. Now it may not have been manifested yet but when it comes you will know. All confusion ceases, selfishness is gone and our sleep is peaceful. God may show us His plan and He may not but than it is okay. For He has all under His control. Like the songwriter said, "We will understand it better by and by." Yes it is a sacrifice, and sacrifice hurts but when we finally let go we begin to see why God requested it in the first place. It is becoming more like His Son Jesus Christ, that was a huge tab and He wasn't the one that ran up the bill but someone had to pay it. God sacrificed His only begotten Son, "For God so loved the world that **He gave** His only begotten Son, that whosoever believeth on Him shall not perish but have everlasting life." And when the time arrived His son followed His father's same example **and gave** his life. Jesus was a seed and God planted Him in the earth. But have we ever wondered what God felt? We already know what Jesus felt when His time came, He prayed to His Father three times and said if it be possible, let this cup pass from me but than changed His mind and said, for this is the reason I came. Not my will but thine be done. So in other words, sacrifice is love. We are set free the very first moment we accept the act of love Jesus displayed on the cross. So presenting our bodies as a living sacrifice holy and acceptable unto Him which is our reasonable service is an act of love.

You see love is free, love is a sacrifice, love is a seed, it is important we understand this. Because if we misunderstand this we would mishandle this precious gift of life. How well am I handling borrowed things? Don't treat the earth like garbage or the people within it because when you do so you are doing it to God. They belong to the most High God and if I shorthand you, I shorthand God. If I cheat you, lie to you, mishandle you...I'm doing it to God. So in other words...be very careful how you handle His seeds.

We are seeds

Are you a participant or a spectator? When God planted us in the earth what did we do or what are we doing? We learned that what is planted will eventually die but than new life springs forth. We tried it this way and it worked for awhile and then died, don't give up try again. Fancy you telling me that Val, yes, guilty as charged but I began again. It doesn't matter how long it takes, try again. Do it again, get excited again, dream again, try it another way just don't stay dead. I need you, I need your fruit to live, I want to live again. How about you?The thing with that is what we did before won't work this time around, like Bishop Jakes preached, "My new normal," the old normal is not working anymore. Yes, I listen to alot of Bishop Jakes teachings for that is how I grow. God's word does the work but he uses the Bishop to expound and I thank God for the man of God and his ministry. May God continue to bless him and all that concerns him. More fruit will come out of this one, so there is a need for more water, more sun light, it would take more effort, more planning, more time, more strategizing, more hands, more help, more support, more of you. Giving of ourselves, availability. What is it that God gave you that you are willing to give? Do you think it could help someone? Do you think it would help the earth? Than give it and when you give it, God will supply you with more. You are life and we need life to live on, give yourself. Give your talents, give your gifts, we need it. If you are a commedian, give it, we need it. Laughter is good for the soul, we need merriment. You could cook liver without it tasting like liver, give the recipe, I need it. Liver is good for you but the flavor throws me off. The earth needs it, we are all connected. Long ago I use to hear the saying about mother earth, never really got into it until later on when I stepped into gardening. Now I'm not a professional yet, I just enjoy doing it and learning from it. But looking at the earth closely, I began to respect it. The earth is submissive and obedient, she's silent and never complains. She has all these insects crawling in and over her and she is steadfast. She gets rained on, men walk all over her yet she's faithful and patient and still brings forth. And so what am I doing to contribute to the family? Am I caring for mother earth and caring for her children? God is the Father and we are His children, am I loving on my syblings? Am I doing my part?

We walk by faith

Not an easy principle to carry out when everything is going haywired before your very eyes. When you are way in over your head and have countless responsiblities. God has placed you in this position or has allowed you to take this course. What is His agenda? To make you more like Christ. Jesus went to His Father to pray quite often when He was on earth, we are to do the same. Things can become very hectic in just a period of moments when just an hour ago it was peaceful. "Lord...I need you now." **Now faith,** not later faith or tomorrow faith or even yesterday's faith but now faith is the substance of things hoped for, the evidence of things not seen. Substance is something we can grab on to, something you could hold to, something you could add to something else. God made Himself substance when He came down to earth, He put on flesh. We was able to touch Him and He was able to touch us. Touch as in knowing what we go through in a human aspect. He knows what it is to suffer, to supply a need for hungry men and women. He knows how it is to lose a best friend and feel sympathy for the people involved... remember Lazarus? Mary and Martha was the sisters of Lazarus and he was very sick and eventually died. The sisters were sadden and that effected Jesus and made him wept, read it for yourself in Saint John chapter 11. How hurtful it is to say goodbye even though we are to see each other again. He knows, He knows, He knows...so let us go to the person that knows it all and does not have a problem telling us how to solve the situation at hand. Looking at Mary when Martha was making the house ready for the guests, Mary sat at the feet of Jesus to hear what He had to say and what she needed to know. The word of God says that He is slow to anger and longsuffering. My questions maybe tedious and long drawn out to a scholared bible teacher but to God it is the perfect opportunity to grow my faith and become more intimate with Him. And the bonus to that is, He never sleeps or slumbers. I don't have to worry about God yawning when I'm talking to Him.

He is a very present help in the time of trouble and not. He is nigh to our mouths, He is closer than we could ever imagine. He won't get angry when we ellaborate on the question to get the answer because we can't comprehend it. The bible says, in all that we get get an understanding. But if I don't understand, how will I be able to carry out what God wants me to do? How can I properly follow leadership if I don't understand? The bible says to obey them that have the rule over you. Lord, you have rule over me. You said as much as lieth in me to get along peaceably with all men but what is happening is creating havoc. And so we have all these things to follow yet lack how to go about it sometimes. Where do we go? To the professional. He is the head, the one in charge... go to God.

He said to diligently seek Him, and so if I'm seeking you then I'm expected to find you. And when we find Him we can boldly come to Him and ask. He said, ask and it shall be given, seek and you shall find, knock and it will be open to you. We can ask the questions: Well what do you mean by this? I don't get this scripture, what did you mean when you said...? How can I do this when that...? Go to the professional. Going to the professional requires faith, I believe you are going to tell me the truth. He said that He is the way, the truth, and the life. We need life, I believe you know what you are doing and have done it before. I can trust you to lead me through the steps, I have never taken this way before. It is written faith without works is dead but how do we work it? Go to God in prayer, go to the word of God and look up the word **work**. Going to a professional is always best, there are friends and family that may be there to assist you but they need God just like me. They need direction just like me, they need help just like me, and so seek God first and let Him lead you. But seek ye first the kingdom of God and His righteousness and all things things shall be added unto you. That answer may come from an individual but you want to go to the right one first. Let God lead you, He knows every persons heart, motive, agenda, mindset and ability; He made them, He knows.

Got a good idea? Do it

You are the only one that will stop you. It is what you allow to stop you. The bible says, you ran well but who did hinder you from obeying the truth. Jesus is the truth, obey Jesus, follow Jesus. Notice the word allow, allow is access. Who are you giving access to your dreams and thoughts? Will that motivate you or will it deplete and fade away? It is all up to you, all our ideas come from who we are. We are made in God's image and likeness. God is the creator, He thought it, spoke it and it came to be. You and I are the same way. He said in the beginning, Let us make man in our image and likeness...we are like God. We create just like God, we speak and it will come. Life and death is in the power of the tongue. Are we speaking life or death? Have you ever heard, "Create the admosphere," well there you have it. What was the outcome after you prayed and spoke out, things changed didn't it? We are receptors, we receive what someone says rather verbally or by expression. After that it is up to you, what will be the outcome? What was that verse that said write the vision and make it plain, that they may run and not faint. You woud be surprise who would downcast your idea but then later on use it. When is it safe to share your ideas and dreams? Who are your boosters? Who are your critics? Is the critic your booster in disguise? Hmm something to think about. Let him who stold steal no more. The thief comes to steal, kill and to destroy if we let it. How do we protect ourselves? God is a strong tower and if you are a child of God, your life is in His hands. The bible says no man could take us out of His hands. So if I'm in His hands then I have no worry, I am protected.

Doubters are really darers, I will give you a few examples: "You sure God told you that?" "I dare you." "You can't do that." "Yea right." "Sure," then they laughed under their breath. "Show me..." They are really saying you can do it. I'm afraid to do it but I know you can do it...and that might mean you will leave me and go forward but I know you could do it. I won't chance it but I know you will, go for it. A dreamer can speak to another dreamer and they will get excited, a dreamer can speak to a spectator and get a different response. Be careful who you hang around, my brother often says, "Association brings on assimilation." In other words, bad communicaton corrupts good manners, especially long periods of time. Don't despise small beginnings...go for it. You have nothing to lose but alot to gain, you will be surprised of the out come.

Full plate

Have you ever ate at a buffet and they had all your favorite foods? And what did you do? Put it all on one plate, I know. And so you have all these good foods but half way through your meal you begin to experience the weight of them all. Did you eat in a hurry or did you pace yourself? Either way you felt the glory of each dish and you would fill bad to throw it away. So how can we make this scenero better? **<u>Take on what you could handle</u>**, take your time, count the cost or should I say calories, and you won't have to worry about wasting anything. So we wrap it up to take home. I thank God for the balance, God is doing a great work in my life I tell you. I prayed for balance in every area of my life. Not just to be a good steward over His finacnces but in everything. My body is the temple of the Holy Ghost and if I destroy it what am I saying to Him? So I balance my life with getting plenty of rest, eating healthy, having fun, making time for my family, keeping God first by spending quality time with Him, getting a good nights sleep, do alot of walking and climbing stairs. I don't have a membersip for a gym but I make sure I walk and dance alot. Laugh and worry about nothing, like Yolanda Adams says on her radio time. Balanced meals are now being explored and it all comes from God. You do know that I'm not just talking food and exercise.

No servant is greater than its master

Understanding ministry as the days progress. Jesus was asleep on that boat when the winds was boisterous. It may look like Jesus didn't care but look again He was full of care. Jesus was full of compassion and concern, virtue leaves your body when you minister to people. Jesus ministered to multitudes, I don't know about you but I would have been asleep myself. When ministering you will need to rest up, eat right, get plenty of sleep, excercise, commune with the Father (prayer), study the word of God, and do something fun...that is the only way you will be able to last through this wonderful journey we call ministry. And most importantly...fast. Apostle Anderson used to say this in his sermons, "If you fast, you will last." That's definitely true, for I do it myself and it works. Another is help, Luke 5: 7 "And they beckoned unto their partners, which were in the other ship, that they should come and help them. And they came, and filled both the ships, so that they began to sink." Jesus said he will make us fishers of men if we follow him. Being a fisherman is a tedious and rewarding job all at once but you can't do it by yourself, you need help. Now I can hear someone saying, the bible says we could do all things through Christ that strengthens us. Yes we could but it also says in Proverbs to use wisdom as your kinsman. Remember Jethro spoke to Moses about what he was doing wasn't wise. Moses was in ministry, the children of Isreal was his congregation and there was no help. Jethro advised his son in law and Moses took heed, read Exodus 18:13-26.

Just because you're tired in your body that doesn't make you forgetful. Now that could happen if you become exhausted and burned out. When you're overly tired your judgement is off, your thinking is distorted, you can't remembered what you just said or if you said anything at all. It doesn't change your identity, you know who you are and your enemy does too yet he tries to convince you otherwise. Like when Charles Stanley used the illustration H.A.L.T.

which consists of: don't allow yourself to get too hungry, too angry, too lonely or too tired, those are the moments of weakness. Then often times to none you begin to experience guilt, which is false guilt but because your discernment is off due to weariness, that gives the devil the foothold. Then you begin to question yourself, I've should have done this, why didn't I just do that and we get up to try to fix things instead of putting it in God's hands and all the while not getting what is truly needed...rest. Resting our bodies and mind causes us to release all in God's care. When we do otherwise, worry shows up and our mind is not on Christ but on the situation: Let this mind be in you which was also in Christ Jesus. The mind of Christ was in control, he had the mind of the Father.

When you get a good night's rest, it makes the world of difference. Remember how the devil tempted Jesus in the wilderness those forty days of fasting...virtue left the body. He wasn't doing a partial fast yet Jesus didn't forget who he was, the word of God...it is written. The word of God became flesh and dwelt among us. You get what I'm saying? So now I'm beginning to see clearly, I was blinded to how and what ministry really is. Ministry is people, pouring in their lives by your everyday living. Talking, sharing, listening, loving, giving, helping, holding, lifting, carrying, encouraging, praying, interceeding, visiting, spending quality time with the ones you love and learning to love, meeting new people...one word...availability. Availability requires all the essentials of staying healthy. You see on the outside looking in and all is glamerous and well put together but we don't get the full picture until we really step into those shoes. There is more to ministry than you know and now that I am on the inside... oh I can see clearly now. Thank you Lord for sending the comforter and thank you comforter for remaining. My hat goes off to those that took place in my life of growth, just to name a few: Overseer Knight, Pastor Adriene, Bishop Blue, Apostle Goings, Bishop Jakes, Bishop Marvin Winans, Pastor Irving, Pastor Garnett, the now deceased Bishop Barber, Bishop Morris, Bishop Johnson, Mother Miller, Deacon Miller, and there are so many more...I was blind but now I see.

Walking in the shoes

I now see through my parents and former pastors eyes, the choices they were forced to make to accommodate all was not always understood or accepted, especially by my hand. I remember sitting in this particular service, it was a special one because the senior bishop was present and teaching about ministry. He made a comment that got my attention. He said, "Just wait until you get there." Now that could have been exciting to another person, there was a great number of people in the audience but when I got the message I knew exactly what God was saying. See at that time I was doing alot of complaining and murmuring. Not to others but to one in particular...my best friend. My best friend is the Savior of all...Jesus, and apparently He got tired of hearing me bicker about what I didn't like. So now that I am there, well have been there for sometime my eyes just weren't open. He opened my eyes and Oh Baby, I had some appologizing to do. I had no idea...not by a long shot. But now that it is me what would be your response? Seek God's instructions, do as He orders and keep my comments to myself. More than likely that was theirs too.

Remember the shoe store Buster Brown? They had shoes that had good quality, durability, long lasting and yes you guessed it very expensive. My mom use to go there to buy my shoes, you see I had very flat feet and I couldn't wear any old shoe. My feet where also turned in and that if it was a pretty shoe by the time it got on my foot the appearance would change, the shoe would look like a boat. I couldn't understand why my sister was able to get the pretty shoes and I had to wear the special ones. They weren't ugly, they were just different. It wasn't one heel higher than the other, they were just different. Alot of times we want what others have but that is not for you. And so I would follow behind my sister and she would pick up the pretty shoes and ask if they had her size and of course they would. It would be a list of shoes she liked and when she placed it on her foot it would fit like a dream. She would occassionally ask me what

I thought and I would tell her it looks good but she wasn't sure and tried on another. While waiting for the next shoe fitting I would look at the other shoes and tell my mom that I liked certain ones and she would let me try them on. The shoe salesman would sit on the mirrored seat and place a sock on my foot to measure it. When he came back I would be so excited, the fresh shoe smell once the box opened, the salesman would remove the shoe horn or white paper and then carefully place the shoe on my foot. My smile would lighten up the whole store, "It fits, it fits." I just thought about Cinderella's sisters when the king's servant placed the shoe on their foot. My mom would smile with me and say, "Let him put on the other one." **The true test would be standing in them.** Sitting in the shoe meant nothing, of course it fits and looked good, how about standing and walking in them.

Then I would hear the familiar line, "Let's try something else," but I know what that meant. It would be excitement all through the store, boxes handing over and being retrieved and then it was my turn. <u>My mom would pick the shoe and place it on my foot</u>. And now I see what God was saying to me, He knows exactly what will fit. There were no openings, no gapping in the middle, and the appearance never changed. When the shoe salesman and mother told me to walk across the floor I would notice the smile on their faces. All was excited and chattered away, "The shoes looks perfect... and you look good too...don't you like them Valerie?" My countenance would be downcasted but my sister had a way of changing things around and by the time we left the store I was happy I got the shoes. What was the point of this story? Wanting ministry for as long as I could remember, there was alot of waiting when I couldn't see why. The ministry I wanted was shepherding but those shoes didn't fit, although I tried them on and was able to walk in them... it just wasn't for me. And now that I can admit that, it was easy to let go and be who God created me to be...just be Valerie. God has invested so much in me and now that I've accepted it, I can flow in the ministry He made just for me. I tell you, the things we learn along the way. I would often hear, "Not now." I had many tutors and governors like the scripture says in the bible but I still wanted it and I wanted it now. And now I see, God is so good...He allowed me to assist in different functions concerning the shepherd and sheep but when the opportunity arrived, I realized that I wasn't excited to be in that position. When the opportunity arrived and the floor was open, they were practically giving it away but I didn't want it. If anything they were more like forcing me to take it, God doesn't force you. Sitting down and placing it on my foot looked good but when it came to walking in it, I noticed the work. And everything consists of work but it would have been sad to be doing something you have no passsion for. Don't get me wrong, I'm passionate about God and people, I just want to be in the right place doing the right thing with the right heart. God sees the heart right? Would He have gotten the glory? No. So now I am doing what I love to do and flowing in it to boot. Taking the box off of God and letting Him have His way in me.

Living the Dream

Dreams do come true, the bible says: Delight yourself in the Lord and He will give you the desires of your heart. I am in my dream and living out my desire. God is so good, he hears our prayers and knows our hearts. He says, I know the thoughts I think towards you thought of good and not evil to give you a hope and an expected end. And in the third book of John he calls us beloved. The second verse reads, that he wishes above all that we will prosper, be in health, even as our souls prosper. Just the thought of God thinking of us brings a smile on my face. He cares, He loves, He knows, He understands, He gives good gifts, He is a good Father and just like any good father he knows what we could handle and take. Although I'm living my dream, I noticed that it takes work to maintain it. Just because it's your dream, that doesn't make it easy. You've got to work that thing and maintain it. And although it gets hard, you still love it and look forward to the next moment. Now that is when He gets the glory. I use to sing this song to the Lord, He didn't have to do it but He did. He didn't have to grant it but He did. He didn't have to hear me but He did. And I am so grateful. The song He gave me to sing to Him was from Him, and just to think...we were touching and agreeing. :)

I'm doing what I love. I'm living what I love. And I am spending it with the ones I love. God is love. Perfect love does cast out all fear. It took love for me to start back to writing again. I haven't written a book in ages. Was I afraid? Could have been but I didn't see it. My first book was full of mistakes and I went through multiple challenges, criticism, people arguing over why they didn't get a book, why they wasn't first, this person got it free why do I have to pay for mine...it was crazy but I tell you, God has a way that is mighty sweet. Now get this, I was waiting on God and He was waiting on me... all this time we were waiting on each other. And when I thought it was too late, it wasn't... it starts when we take that first step. All this time I thought I had writers block. I write all the time, how can I have writers block? I tell you... it's mindset. What was I telling myself? You do know that it starts with a thought. And when a thought sets in, it goes to the heart, and what is embedded in the heart the mouth speaks. What are you telling yourself? Live your dream, it's not too late. It's not over...its just begun. It's a new season, it's a new day...a fresh anointing is coming your way. It's a season of power and prosperity, it's a new season and its coming for me (put your name here.) Like the song writer says, "This is my season for grace and favor." Do you believe it? Remember when those that came to Jesus for healing, he said to them, "Do you believe I can do this?" And they responded, Yeah Lord. And He said, "According unto your faith let it be done unto you." So, do you believe God can do this? According to your faith let it be done unto you. God is so good. I love Him.

Read it Slow and aloud

Have you ever read the word of God (the bible) slowly? You should try it, it makes the world of a difference especially if you read it aloud. You actually hear what God is saying, and faith comes by hearing and hearing the word of God. One of my former pastors said to read the bible like you never read it before and I took that offer and applied it to my own life and it made a difference. Let's try a few verses: For God so loved the world that He gave His only begotten Son, that whosoever believeth in Him shall not perish but have everlasting life. For God so loved the world, let's look at that first. For God so loved, so loved is in love. I so love you, no matter what you do I so love you. I don't agree with what you do but I so love you that I'm going to give you my son. I love my son, He is my only son but I love you and he can help you, so I'm giving him away to the world. What consists of the world? People...there are many people in the world. I've heard the strangest arguments come across in my christian walk, how they encourage others to do away with the world but God so loved the world. You want to do away with what God so loves? Does that make any sense? You love God but want to do away with the world. Moving right along....Okay, so let us look at the whosoever...all of us is the whosoever. Whosoever....who ever believes in Him, it is not hard to believe. Either you believe Him or you don't. Whosoever believeth on Him shall not perish but have everlasting life. Now why should God lie? If He said it then it is so, all that matters is what God says to you and what you say to yourself. Saying what God says brings life. Agreeing with God brings life. You are touching and agreeing with God what He is saying to you. You shall have everlasting life... Jesus came that I\we may have life and have it more abundantly. Abundance is plentiful and everlasting is eternal, immortal, it doesn't run out, it never ends. So what God is saying? My life would never run out, that your life will never run out.

Here is another one: Isaiah 53 : 5 (KJV) "But He was wounded for our transgressions, he was bruised for our iniquities: the chastisement of our peace was upon Him, and by His stripes we are healed." He was wounded for our, who is the our? We are the our. Transgression, you broke the law but because I love you I'm going to get the beating. I'm going to take the punishment because I love you. You deserve it but you can't handle it so I'm going to handle it for you. Bruised for our iniquities, our iniquities...not His but our, remember we are the our. He got black and blue, busted up, wounds are open cuts, bruises are discolored lumps that was brought about with instruments to and blows to His body. Iniquities is wickedness, so He got beaten for our wickedness not His because there is no wickedness in God. The chastisement of our peace was upon Him. If that is not love, I don't know what love is. Come on, punishment was inflicted upon someone that loves the world so much...that you and I may have peace. And not just peace but eternal life. And by His stripes we are healed...so before I got the fractured foot I was already healed. Before you got the stroke you were already healed. Before the sickness came you were already healed. Before you went to the doctor you were already healed. **You are already healed**...no matter what comes you are already healed. No matter what we have to travel through...we are already healed. What heals us? Believing the work Jesus did on earth and the cross. You may have been in the bed for a period of years but I came to remind you of God's word...You are already healed. Remember the man that sat at the pool for 38 years and Jesus asked him, "Do you want to be made well?" This is found in the book of John the fifth chapter. The seventh verse says, "The sick man answered Him, Sir, I have no man to put me into the pool when the water is stirred up, but while I am coming, another steps down before me." Now get this, verse eight and nine says, "Jesus said unto him, Rise, take up your bed and walk. And immediately the man was made well, took up his bed, and walked. And that day was the Sabbath." God is the same yesterday, today and forever more...He changes not. If He did it before He can do it again. His methods may change but God never changes. Forever never ends people, it never ends. It goes on and on like space, space doesn't end and neither does God.

James 1: 17 (Guideons) "Every good gift and every perfect gift is from above, and comes down from the Father of lights, with whom there is no variation or shadow of turning." This verse is self explanitory, God doesn't change His mind, He is not an Indian giver. If He gives you a gift, He doesn't take it back. The gift is yours, it's our responsibility is to take care of it. And the blessings of the Lord maketh rich and addeth no sorrow. If you got sorrow, that is not from the Lord. If you are greiving me, that is not from the Lord. If you are stressing me, that is not from the Lord. The devil comes to steal, kill and to destroy...if it is robbing you of your joy it is not of the Lord. That is not a gift that is a curse, let go of the curse and stay blessed of the Lord. Matthew 7: 7 - 11 (Guideons) "Ask, and it will be given to you, seek and you will find, knock and it will be opened to you. For everyone who asks receives, and he who seeks finds, and to him who knocks it will be opened. Or what man is there among you who, if his son asks bread, will give him a stone? Or if he asks for a fish will give him a serpent? If you then being evil, know how to give good gifts to your children, how much more will your Father who is in heaven give good things to those who ask Him!"

I would say the end but it is not, for it has just begun. Thank you to all of my readers, it has been a pleasure to serve you in this capacity. May the Lord continue to bless you, strengthen you and give you peace.

Forever yours, Valerie